A Day at the Petting Zoo

Un día en el zoológico interactivo

I0806566

THIS EDITION
Produced for DK by WonderLab Group LLC
Jennifer Emmett, Erica Green, Kate Hale, *Founders*

Editor Maya Myers; **Photography Editor** Kelley Miller; **Managing Editor** Rachel Houghton; **Designers** Project Design Company; **Researcher** Michelle Harris; **Copy Editor** Lori Merritt; **Indexer** Connie Binder; **Proofreader** Susan K. Hom; **Spanish Translation** Isabel C. Mendoza; **Proofreader of the Spanish text** Carmen Orozco; **Series Reading Specialist** Dr. Jennifer Albro

First American Edition, 2023
Published in the United States by DK Publishing, a division of Penguin Random House LLC
1745 Broadway, 20th Floor, New York, NY 10019

25 26 27 10 9 8 7 6 5 4 3 2 1
001-345923-August/2025

Published in Great Britain by Dorling Kindersley Limited

A catalog record for this book is available from the Library of Congress.
HC ISBN: 978-0-5939-6659-4
PB ISBN: 978-0-5939-6658-7

Printed and bound in China
Super Readers Lexile® levels BR40L to 300L (English text)

The publisher would like to thank the following for their kind permission to reproduce their images:
a=above; c=center; b=below; l=left; r=right; t=top; b/g=background
Dreamstime.com: Adogslifephoto 8bl; **Fotolia:** Anatolii 13br; **Shutterstock.com:** Blur Life 1975 16c, narikan 15c, Hayk_Shalunts 26c, shupian 30, Studio 11 20c

Cover images: *Front:* **Dreamstime.com:** Blue Ring Education Pte Ltd (grass), Arif Budiyana (clouds), Evgenii Naumov (fences); **Shutterstock.com:** Rita_Kochmarjova b; *Back:* **Dreamstime.com:** Gunel Abbasova clb, Colorfuelstudio cra, Pavel Naumov cla; *Spine:* **Shutterstock.com:** Rita_Kochmarjova

www.dk.com

FSC www.fsc.org MIX Paper | Supporting responsible forestry FSC™ C018179

This book was made with Forest Stewardship Council™ certified paper – one small step in DK's commitment to a sustainable future.
Learn more at
www.dk.com/uk/information/sustainability

Pre-level

A Day at the Petting Zoo

Un día en el zoológico interactivo

DK

We are at the petting zoo.

Estamos en el zoológico interactivo.

We are petting a donkey.

Estamos acariciando a un burro.

donkeys

burros

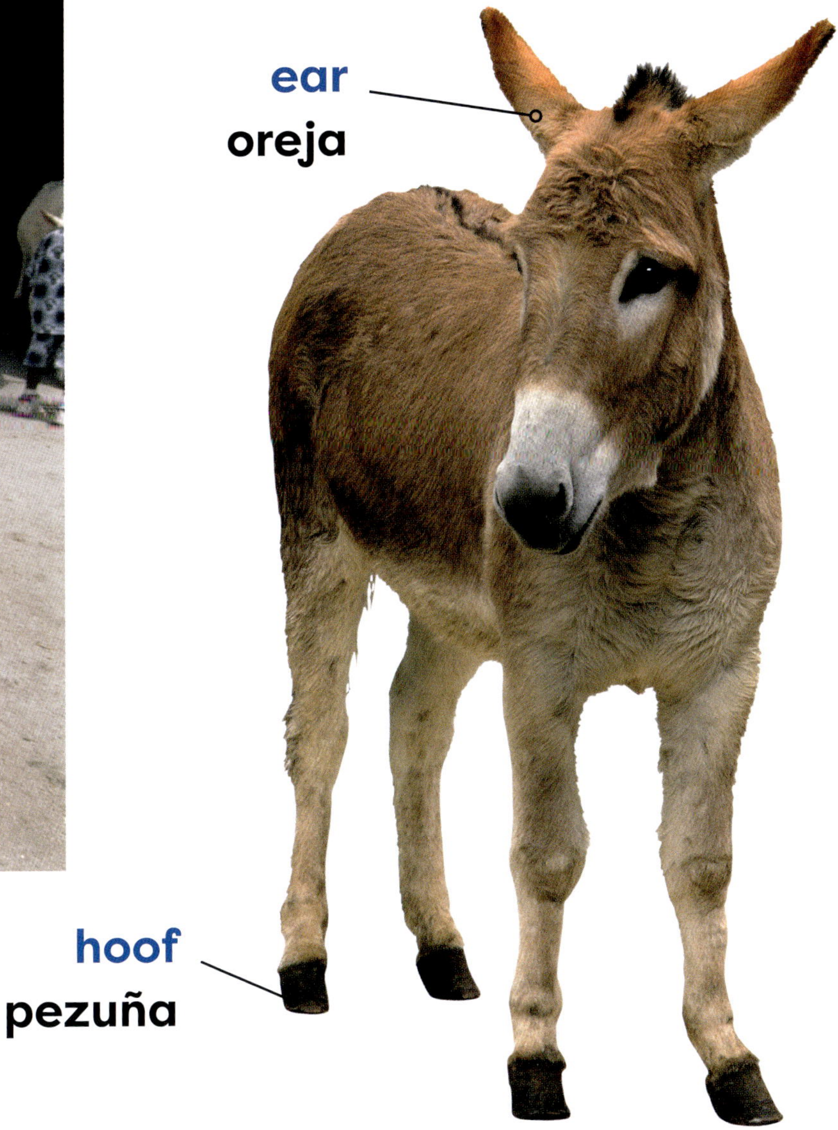
ear
oreja
hoof
pezuña

We are walking two baby llamas.

Estamos paseando a dos crías de llama.

llamas

llamas

leash
correa

I am brushing a pony.

Estoy cepillando a un poni.

ponies and horses

ponis y caballos

mane
crin

pigs and piglets

cerdos y lechones

I am picking up a little pink piglet.

Estoy cargando a un lechoncito rosado.

hen

gallina

chicks

pollitos

I am holding a soft yellow chick.

Tengo en mis manos un suave pollito amarillo.

I am carrying a green stick insect.

Tengo en mi mano un insecto palo verde.

stick insects

insectos palo

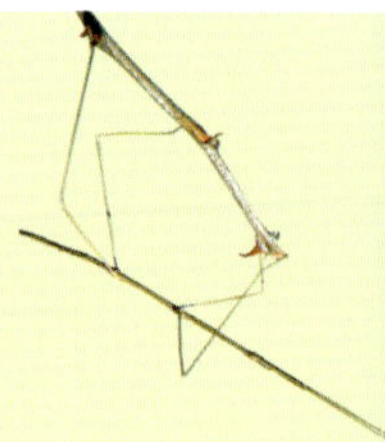

leaf
hoja
stick insect
insecto palo

frogs

ranas

I am watching
a beady-eyed frog.

Estoy mirando a una
rana de ojos saltones.

Ribbit! Ribbit!
¡Croac! ¡Croac!

It is mealtime now. I am giving the woolly lamb some milk.

Ya es la hora de comer. Le estoy dando leche al lanudo cordero.

lambs

corderos

wool
lana

rabbits

conejos

I am feeding a hungry rabbit.

Yo le estoy dando de comer a un hambriento conejo.

This fluffy guinea pig
is eating a leaf.

Este peludo cobaya se está
comiendo una hoja.

guinea pigs

cobayas

whiskers
bigotes
claws
garras

The white goose wants a snack.

El ganso blanco quiere
una merienda.

geese

gansos

feathers
plumas
bill
pico

goats

cabras

This long-horned goat is eating his lunch.

Esta cabra de cuernos largos se está comiendo su almuerzo.

Goodbye, animals!
It is time to go home.

¡Adiós, animales!
Es hora de irse a casa.

Glossary
Glosario

donkey
a small horse-like animal with long ears

frog
a short animal with long back legs

goose
a large bird with a long neck and a bill

llama
a large, woolly animal from South America

stick insect
a long, thin insect that looks like a stick

burro
animal pequeño parecido a un caballo con orejas largas

ganso
ave grande de cuello largo y pico grueso

insecto palo
insecto largo y delgado que parece un palito

llama
animal grande y lanudo de América del Sur

rana
animal corto que tiene las patas traseras largas

Quiz
Prueba

Answer the questions to see what you have learned. Check your answers with an adult.

Which animal am I?

1. I am a fluffy animal with a long neck and pointed ears.
2. I am a pink animal with hooves and a snout.
3. I am a woolly baby sheep.
4. I am a bird with a long neck and a bill.
5. I have long horns and big, floppy ears.

1. A llama 2. A pig 3. A lamb 4. A goose 5. A long-horned goat

Responde las preguntas para saber cuánto aprendiste. Verifica tus respuestas con un adulto.

¿Qué animal soy?

1. Soy un animal peludo de cuello largo y orejas puntudas.
2. Soy un animal rosado con pezuñas y hocico.
3. Soy una oveja pequeña y lanuda.
4. Soy un ave de cuello largo y pico grueso.
5. Tengo unos cuernos largos y unas orejas grandes y blandas.

1. Una llama 2. Un cerdo (o un lechón) 3. Un cordero 4. Un ganso
5. Una cabra de cuernos largos